What

MW01488869
Needs to Know About

Leading in a Congregation

Michael A. Bealla

DISCIPLESHIP RESOURCES

PO BOX 340003 • NASHVILLE, TN 37203-0003
www.discipleshipresources.org

Cover and book design by Joey McNair

Edited by Linda R. Whited and David Whitworth

ISBN 0-88177-435-9

DR435

Contents

Introduction

Congregations identify leaders all the time. Someone is named to chair a committee, for instance, or asked to guide a task force. There are many reasons that individuals have a leadership position. Some leaders are chosen because they know about the work the committee will do. Others are asked to serve because of their faithful commitment to the congregation. Some people agree to lead simply because the job needs to be done and no one else will do it. Some leaders emerge because of their professional and secular experience; others emerge because their lives display the fruits of deep faith.

Effective ministry calls for leaders who combine both skills and faith. Effective ministry calls for spiritual leaders. Spiritual leadership is a life of growth. Spiritual leaders continually increase their practical leading skills while deepening their relationship with God.

The booklets in this *What Every Leader Needs to Know About . . .* series are about being a spiritual leader. Each booklet has basic information for the growth of spiritual leaders in congregations. Some booklets in the series focus on people skills and others focus on spiritual practices, yet each one brings these two facets of leadership together. There are other resources apart from this series that outline job descriptions and models for specific ministries. Some of those helps are listed in the bibliographies of these booklets.

Spiritual leadership suggests that every leadership experience includes the possibility of life-changing transformation. It may be that the leader's life is transformed. It may be that the committee or task force becomes a faith community in which God's presence is known. It may be that the product or project of the work transforms the congregation and the world. Spiritual leadership expresses the hope that God's transforming love will infuse individual lives, small groups, congregations, and the world.

"Do not be conformed to this world, but be transformed by the renewing of your minds.... Let love be genuine" (Romans 12:2, 9).

Betsey Heavner
Director, Congregational Leader Formation

Wanted: Spiritual Leaders

Do you remember the story? Moses was minding his own business. Actually, he was minding his father-in-law's sheep business when he received his "call." A voice spoke from a bush that was on fire but was not being consumed. "Moses! I have listened to the cries of my people in Egypt. I have a job for you. I want you to lead my people from captivity to freedom" (see Exodus 3).

Suddenly, Moses found himself called by God in the midst of his life, complicated as it had been in earlier days, to be about God's business. Called ... chosen by the One who knew him best, flaws and all, to become a leader in order to deliver God's people to new life.

I suspect your first sense of call from God was to discipleship. Perhaps it came as an invitation to become a part of the family of God, which we call the church. Or maybe you felt a strong desire to help other people. However the invitational call came to you, you said "yes!"

As you walked your journey of faith, your local church

helped you to experience the powerful presence of God in worship, the support of community, and the joy of service. You were nurtured in discipleship and began to hear God's call as a continuing and deeper claim on your life.

Then, one day while you were simply minding your own business, you received a call to serve as a leader in your congregation. Now, while that call was more likely experienced through the voice of a member of the lay leadership committee and lacked the drama of a burning bush and a voice from within it, I dare to suggest that your call to lead was as real as the call Moses experienced!

This call is not new. It seems God has a long history of calling into spiritual leadership and servanthood people who were simply minding their everyday business. Recognizing their faith, their gifts, and their leadership potential, God called out Noah, Abraham and Sarah, Jeremiah, Isaiah, Mary, Peter, James, and John from among others to serve or lead God's people.

With an ever-growing focus on faith formation, the church needs not just leaders but *spiritual* leaders. Spiritual leaders understand they are called—they are not volunteers! Volunteers offer to help on their own and feel free to walk away if the journey gets too tough. But spiritual leaders respond to God's call, which connects them in covenant with both God and the community that has placed trust in their leadership.

Since you are reading this booklet, others have obviously seen in you the necessary gifts and potential for leading in your congregation. They have been moved by the Holy

Spirit to call you forth to lead them. Please remember! You are called!

Called to Spiritual Leadership

1. Take a few moments to think about your own life with God. Do you remember when God first called you to be a member of God's church? Were you a child or an adult? How did you know that God was calling you?

_____

_____

_____

_____

_____

2. Who were the people through whom you heard God's call? What did they say or do?

_____

_____

_____

_____

_____

3. Do you believe that God has "called" you into your leadership position? What is the difference between being called and volunteering?

_____

_____

_____

_____

_____

4. What was the first leadership role you filled in the church as a whole? In your current congregation?

_____

_____

_____

_____

_____

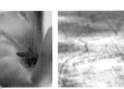

Me? A Spiritual Leader?

The world has changed, to be sure. While the purpose of the church remains the same, the need for spiritual leaders to emerge from within our churches has never been more critical. Many believe the church's future will depend on whether or not we can more intentionally call forth and grow spiritual leaders who understand the church's role as a faith-forming community. Such leaders need more than ordinary leadership skills. They also need to lead from the personal spiritual center that God has placed within them.

By now you might be asking, "Why me?" Perhaps like Moses you may be gathering up your excuses to explain to God that there are several hundred better choices for spiritual leaders than you.

One after the other, God turned down each of Moses' best excuses. When Moses suggested he needed to know who it was that was sending him—"Just who is God? What is God's name?"—God explained that God had always been and always would be, but offered Moses a name anyway, "I am who I am," as a starting point (Exodus 3:13-15).

Next, Moses suggested the people might not believe he had the skills or abilities to lead. God had an answer for this one as well. Moses was given a staff (no, not three advisors; a *wooden* staff) to symbolize his calling and authority. In essence God promised Moses the necessary tools for leading the people to freedom and the promise of God's presence (Exodus 4:1-5).

Moses tried one last time to offer God a chance to call someone else. He quite eloquently explained to God that he could not speak well, being slow of tongue and speech. So God offered him a solution, a team member, his brother Aaron, who God explained had all the necessary eloquence needed to deliver God's message both to Pharaoh and to God's suffering people (Exodus 4:10-16).

It worked! Moses and Aaron teamed up, clearly understanding their mission, and began the long, hard journey of delivering the people of God. It was not easy to lead, and it took a long time to get there, but eventually the people of God were standing one step away from the Promised Land.

Needless to say, God would not have chosen you to be a spiritual leader in your church if God did not think you were the one for the job! Why you? Why not?!

Yes! You Are a Spiritual Leader

1. When have you felt unprepared to lead in a way that God was calling you to lead? What was lacking?

_____

_____

_____

_____

2. What excuses did you offer to God before you said yes to your leadership role? What moved you to say yes?

_____

_____

_____

_____

_____

3. What tools did you need that you did not have?

_____

_____

_____

_____

4. When have you fearfully said yes to God's call only to find that God supplied what you needed to be a leader?

_____

_____

_____

_____

_____

What Qualities Do Spiritual Leaders Need?

Y ou have encountered gifted people in your congregation who have strong skills for leadership. What is the difference between leading and leading as a spiritual leader?

While there are many attributes of a spiritual leader that can be explored, perhaps the most important of these is that a spiritual leader is first of all one who is centered in Christ. A spiritual leader clearly understands the mission of the church and can state it. He or she helps lift up the vision that God has planted in the hearts and minds of the people. He or she empowers others to share their gifts by modeling shared or team leadership. Spiritual leaders seek a balance between their faith and their leadership skills.

Spiritual leaders also recognize that leadership is not easy. They are aware of their strengths and weaknesses, and they seek to grow both in faith and in skills. They also know that they are not alone. God will raise up "Aarons," providing for team leadership. And of course, they know the God who called them into leadership is walking on the journey with them.

Spiritual Leaders

- are deeply centered in their relationship with Jesus Christ;
- clearly understand the mission of the church;
- help to hold the vision of the congregation before the people;
- know their strengths (gifts) and weaknesses (areas for growth);
- recognize the gifts of those they lead and encourage their use;
- understand the benefits of shared leadership (team ministry);
- know that God is always with them.

A Few Moments to Reflect

Spiritual leaders listen for God in the midst of everyday life. As with the burning bush, sometimes God comes to us in ways we least expect. Being aware of such encounters is important, or else we may think our "burning bush" is just another brush fire and pass on by. Pause for a moment to answer the following questions:

1. What qualities do you need to strengthen in order to become a more effective spiritual leader?

_____

_____

_____

_____

2. How would you describe your call to be in ministry through your church today?

_____

_____

_____

_____

3. What expectations do you have for fulfilling God's call in the future? Is there any specific call that you should be listening to right now?

_____

_____

_____

_____

_____

Practicing Spiritual Leadership

Centered in Christ

The excuses Moses spoke to God offer us an important insight into how to grow as spiritual leaders. When Moses asked God, "What is your name? Who shall I tell the people called me?" he was in essence asking God for a revelation of God's self. Perhaps better put, in order for Moses to lead the people, he needed a deeply centered relationship with the One who was calling him to serve.

Throughout their long and sometimes rocky relationship, Moses and God talked often. Moses would go up a mountain and stay for an extended period of time during which God renewed his strength and helped him grow in faith.

If we are to be effective spiritual leaders today, a strong relationship with God in Christ is essential. Just as two people grow to love each other as they spend time talking and listening to each other, so it is with our relationship with God. Should regular communication be set aside, the relationship weakens, sometimes even to the point of failure.

Enter the Means of Grace

John Wesley, founder of the Methodist movement, taught the importance for all Christian disciples of practicing what he called the "means of grace." Simply put, these are disciplines that help us to encounter the presence, spirit, and power of God. They are like a pipeline to God's resources. They nurture us along our spiritual journeys.

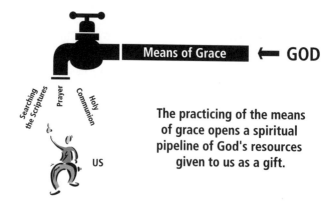

Means of Grace ← **GOD**

Searching the Scriptures   Prayer   Holy Communion

US

The practicing of the means of grace opens a spiritual pipeline of God's resources given to us as a gift.

While the Scriptures point to many such means of grace, among those which Wesley lifted up as being vital to growing in our love of God and deepening our faith were prayer, searching the Scriptures, and Holy Communion. These spiritual "pipelines" are three ways leaders can become "centered in Christ."

Prayer: Private and Public

Daily prayer is vital to discipleship and especially relevant to those committed to spiritual leadership. The setting aside of prayer time provides the means to commune with God. Not only will daily prayer strengthen your faith, which is an important goal for spiritual leaders, but you just might, by the grace of God, fall in love with God in new and deeper ways than ever before.

Remember also that prayer is two-way communication. Do not just offer up a list of your joys and concerns. Listen for God's voice and insight. In our fast-paced culture, we have become much better at transmitting than receiving. Listen for God's still, small voice!

The biblical story witnesses to the renewing, empowering, soul-strengthening, soul-softening, heart-tenderizing power of prayer. Whether we think of Moses going up the mountain to speak to God, Jesus finding a lonely place apart, or the apostle Paul crying out to God from prison, it is clear that such prayer time is absolutely essential if we are to be spiritually grounded and effective in our leadership!

Just as important as private prayer is corporate prayer. Spiritual leaders realize the need to be present in weekly worship. There is a power that flows from the community that cannot be experienced apart from the body of Christ coming together. Worship also reminds leaders of the importance of their task, the good news of the gospel, and the power of God's transforming love. If the apostle Paul is correct, and the church is the body of Christ alive in the world today, and if all of us are members of that body, then the body is only truly whole when every member is present. Spiritual leaders model for the whole body the importance of faithfully worshiping in community.

(For a more complete look at prayer read *What Every Leader Needs to Know About Leading in Prayer,* one of the booklets in this series.)

Searching the Scriptures

A second important means of grace for spiritual leaders centers around the Scriptures. While it may be possible to lead people with only skill knowledge, staying on course requires a knowledge of God's story. Spiritual leaders know the foundational stories of the Old and New Testaments and can use them to gain insight and understanding of God's will that are essential for leading the church.

Since our mission of making disciples in order to transform the world belongs exclusively to the church, knowledge of how to run a business, how to make investments, or even how to work with people will fall short of our task if we do not have a strong knowledge of who we are as God's church. Spiritual leaders must become grounded in God's biblical word.

Remember the "tool" God gave Moses? Moses used that staff as a witness to the power of God. Spiritual leaders can use a tool that Wesley called "searching the Scriptures." Searching the Scriptures is a way of reading, listening, and reflecting on the written word in search of helpful stories, teachings, and human experiences with God that are relevant first to our lives but then also to the work of our committees and the whole church as we seek to do God's will. Spiritual leaders understand why John Wesley sought to be "a man of one book"!

Spending Time at the Table

A third important means of grace for spiritual leaders is Holy Communion. Although there are many ways to think about the nature of Holy Communion, one way is to realize that as the faith community gathers to share the holy meal, the bread is broken or "dis-membered" as a symbol of Christ's self-giving love. Through the bread and cup and the power of the Holy Spirit, we "re-member" the body of Christ. Together we experience the profound sense of Christ's real presence in our "common-unity."

This Holy "Common-union" we share together is an empowering source of grace through which God pours God's self upon us. Spiritual leaders understand that the work of the church is centered in forgiveness and grace and calls for the pouring out of our lives in Christian service.

Prayer, individual and corporate; searching the Scriptures through reading, study, and reflection; and participation in Holy Communion provide spiritual leaders with the faith tools they need to be effective in their leadership roles.

A Moment to Reflect

1. How have you felt the presence of God in prayer, Scripture study, and Holy Communion?

_____

_____

_____

_____

2. If you could strengthen one area of your spiritual life,
    what would it be?

    _____

    _____

    _____

3. What help do you need from your congregation to help
    you feel more confident about being a spiritual leader?
    Who in your congregation can help you strengthen your
    spiritual practices?

    _____

    _____

    _____

    _____

(Another booklet in this series, *What Every Leader
Needs to Know About Leading Meetings,* offers suggestions
for strengthening the spiritual life of the group you lead.)

Rediscovering
Christian Community

Toward the end of the last century a curious practice of isolated living was emerging. Sociologists referred to it as "cocooning." Although this living apart from community has continued for some, more and more people have tired of the isolation and are seeking new connections and community. Such community can be found in service organizations, parent groups, fire companies, fitness clubs, dance clubs, and sports bars. And to be honest, the church cannot always compete with these sources solely in terms of social interaction. As this trend toward connections and community continues, though, the church can no longer afford to blame the culture and say, "the church is not central to people's lives anymore." Rather, we need to find new ways to help people discover the transforming and nurturing power of Christian community. We can do that if we take the time to be sure Christian community is alive and well in our congregations. To paraphrase the theme from a movie of the late 1980's, "If we build it, they will come!"

Although we have learned that people will not come for a building, we have also learned that they will come if we build community. No other organization or community of people in the whole world is given the charge of providing Christian community!

How might we define Christian community? Sometimes it is easier to say what something looks and feels like than to use definitive words. Christian community is clearly centered in Christ. It is fellowship built on sharing our lives as we share a love for Christ. It feels like we belong no matter who we are. It feels safe and accepting. It is a place where people are of value simply because they are children of God.

Christian community is a gift from God. It comes about not by willing it to happen but by providing a grace-filled environment in which the Holy Spirit can work. Bound by our baptismal covenant, we hold one another accountable as we walk the Christian journey. We are encouraged to live in a way that John Wesley called being "made perfect in love." The continuing practice of the means of grace becomes vital as spiritual leaders model for others a life-long journey of faith.

Spiritual leaders ask themselves this vital question on a regular basis: "Whenever people come to our church for any reason, is it clear they are participating in Christian community?"

Christian Community and Your Church

1. When have you felt the love and acceptance of Christian community?

_____

_____

_____

_____

2. What one thing is your church best known for throughout your community? What does that say about your church?

_____

_____

_____

_____

3. Assuming Christian community is alive and well in your church, how can your church reach out to those seeking a connection who may not have thought first of all of the church?

_____

_____

_____

_____

_____

(You can learn more by reading *Cultivating Christian Community,* by Thomas R. Hawkins. See the list of suggested resources on pages 45–48.)

Spiritual Leaders Continue to Grow

As the church makes its way in this twenty-first century, change is occurring around us at a record pace. For the church to continue to be faithful in its mission and ministry, it will need to grow spiritual leaders who are willing to learn and are continually seeking to improve their leadership skills.

Spiritual leaders are always looking for ways to become more effective. They recognize the changing world around them and learn how to help move people through change with as little resistance and pain as possible. They understand that change is part of the creative nature of God. As they try new things or evaluate past efforts, they see successes as gifts along the journey and failures as learning moments. They understand the value of celebrating past accomplishments while being open to God's leading into the future.

Lone Rangers Need Not Apply

Moses learned through God's response to his last excuse that leadership is not an individual task. Aaron shared his gifts for leadership with Moses, and by the time they had led God's people to the edge of the Promised Land, the leaders of the tribes had also become part of the team. A new model of team leadership was born!

Spiritual leaders encourage mutual responsibility in leadership. They depend on those they are called to lead for insight, knowledge, and reflection. They realize that while they are responsible for lifting up the vision of the church before the congregation, they are not the source of the vision. God plants that vision in the hearts and minds of all the people. Spiritual leaders learn to ask the right kinds of questions to others to help discern where God is leading the church.

More than that, they realize that God has given each person in the church special gifts and abilities. Moses was a doer; Aaron was a talker; one gift enhanced another. Spiritual leaders seek to discover their own gifts as well as the gifts of those they are called to lead. In turn, they call on those people to use their gifts for the good of the whole church, and the team model of leadership is given new life.

Have you ever noticed what happens when a person discovers a way to use what he or she loves to do in the church and is set free to do it? Such people experience new meaning and joy in their lives. As they blossom, they just might discover that they too can be spiritual leaders!

Growing Spiritual Leaders in Your Church

1. Where are there examples of team leadership in your church?

_____

_____

_____

_____

_____

2. What gifts and skills do you have for leadership?

_____

_____

_____

_____

_____

3. Have you ever taken a spiritual gifts inventory? You might try the one in *Equipped for Every Good Work,* by Dan R. Dick and Barbara Miller (for more information, see the list of resources at the end of this booklet or visit www.gbod.org/equipped). What can you discover about your own gifts?

_____

_____

_____

_____

4. How might a spiritual gifts inventory be used to help the people you lead?

_____

_____

_____

Don't Get Lost in the Wilderness!

Just a generation ago the thought of a satellite system that could pinpoint someone's location anywhere on the face of the earth seemed like science fiction. But now, with a touch of a button in one's car or by turning on a pocket PC, you can do just that. Imagine, if only Moses and Aaron had had a "GPS" (Global Positioning System) handheld device! Finding the Promised Land would have been a cake walk!

So far, we have looked at the qualities and tasks of spiritual leaders. But you may be wondering how you and your congregation can keep from getting lost in the wilderness of local church life. Is there a tool or a map to help guide your way?

The answer is "Yes!" Earlier we said that a spiritual leader understands the mission of the church. Your congregation may have developed its own mission statement. While every church may have its unique statement, most of them reflect something close to the Great Commission in the Gospel of Matthew (Matthew 28:19-20). A mission statement might be something like

> "The mission of the church is to make disciples
> for Jesus Christ in order to transform the world."

Adopting such a statement as the mission of your church helps guide your work and reminds the various committees, teams, and councils, along with the whole congregation, why the church exists—what business it is in. Too often mission statements are written and may even be printed in the weekly worship bulletin but are then forgotten as the ongoing life of the church continues. Remember that a mission statement is only helpful when it keeps the congregation focused on the reason for its existence. It is the task of spiritual leaders to be faithful in keeping the mission statement as the frame around the church's ministry.

An official mission statement is a good beginning. The church's leaders now have a means by which to measure each activity, process, or program ministry as it fits within that frame. If a ministry helps achieve the stated mission, then the church stays the course. If, however, a ministry or activity falls outside the mission frame, spiritual leaders should raise questions about why the church is doing the activity. (A resource to help with this concept is another booklet in this series, entitled *What Every Leader Needs to Know About Leading With Purpose.*)

While a mission statement clearly defines the church's purpose, another component that is just as important is the picture inside the frame, the vision! Indeed, the writer

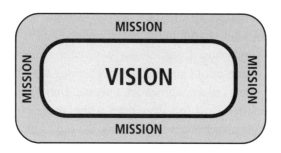

of Proverbs declared that "a people without vision will die" (29:18, paraphrased).

A vision is really a picture of how a congregation will look when its mission is fulfilled. If the mission is to make Christian disciples, then the vision is a picture of how the church will look when that has been done. While churches may share a common mission, each church must develop a vision unique to its own life. As time moves on the vision will change as the realities of that church change. Do not worry! Spiritual leaders see change as God doing something new and inviting the church to share an ever-evolving vision.

As a learning leader you are probably wondering where a church's vision comes from. Again the biblical story holds a clue. While we might be tempted to say Moses had a vision of God's people living free from the oppression of slavery, or even perhaps that God gave Moses that vision of new life to hold before the people, we should realize that God called Moses to the task of delivering God's people because God had heard their cries in captivity (Exodus 3:7-9). The vision is a gift of God placed within the hearts and minds of God's people. God has placed a vision for your church in the hearts and the minds of the people—both those in and those yet to be in the church.

The vision can be discovered by listening to the innermost yearnings of a congregation's people. How can leaders discover what is packed away deep within the people's hearts? Spiritual leaders learn to ask the right questions to discern God's movement in the congregation and the surrounding community. As each person shares his or her innermost spiritual needs, it is as if these sacred treasures are pieces of a puzzle that form a picture when put together. When all the pieces are uncovered and brought together, a spiritual leader can help hold up the completed picture before the people as a shared vision of where God is leading them.

Together, a clearly defined mission and shared vision of the future will be your guidance system and help keep your church from wandering aimlessly in the wilderness.

Just a reminder, however. Sometimes wandering is a necessary part of learning and growing in our faith. It helps us to depend on God. But healthy wandering happens best when it is guided by a mission and a vision!

Pause to Reflect Again

1. Does your congregation have a clearly defined mission statement? If so, write it here.

_____

_____

_____

_____

_____

2. How are the members of your congregation made aware of the church's mission? How can this process be improved? How might their being aware of the mission help keep the church focused?

_____

_____

_____

_____

_____

3. One measure of how well a church is carrying out its mission is the number of people who have come into relationship with your congregation through the profession of faith. How many people have been received into the membership of your congregation by profession of faith during the last year?

_____

_____

4. How can you, as a spiritual leader, help your church stay focused on its mission, keeping "wandering in the wilderness" to a minimum?

_____

_____

One Step From the Promised Land

After more than two years (see Numbers 9:1; 10:11) Moses, Aaron, and the former slaves stood looking across a valley at the Promised Land. Their vision was all but a reality! In Numbers 13 you can read about spies sent into the new land to see what the land was like and what the people might encounter there. The spies brought back a mixed report that left the people divided over whether to move ahead. Some believed the land was the wonderful place that fulfilled God's promise, while others feared that any action would lead to failure. Some were so afraid that they were more willing to go back to the slavery of Egypt or even wander aimlessly in the wilderness than to face the challenge that moving into the Promised Land might bring. The result of their wavering was to wander forty years before reaching the Promised Land (read Numbers 14:34).

Whether you are just beginning your journey in leadership or are a seasoned leader looking to grow, know that challenges lie ahead. Changing the way we lead will raise some questions. Practicing spiritual leadership is a lifelong journey of prayer, reflection, listening, and growing in the knowledge and love of God. A well-meaning finance committee member, upon hearing this description of spiritual leadership, chided, "And I thought I just needed to understand the line items in our budget!"

Shortly after talking with a group of chairpersons about spiritual leadership, a pastor was asked by one of them to close their session with prayer. Instead, she suggested that one of them might offer the prayer this time. After a momentary silence that perhaps implied the pastor was shirking her duty, someone offered a marvelous prayer that sent the group on its way.

A colleague told a story about a board-of-trustees chairperson replacing the opening word of prayer with a brief Scripture lesson and discussion. He reported that for a moment you might have thought everyone had fainted at the idea of taking time for scriptural reflection at a "business" meeting. But as time passed and such devotional moments continued, a new sense of community grew that has nurtured a leadership team that enjoys sharing a portion of their lives as they serve the church.

At first, thinking about spiritual leadership, especially in terms of including spiritual formation as part of our meetings, may raise questions that are more of a reaction to change than a reaction to substance. Someone may ask, "We never did these things as part of our meetings before. Have we been doing it all wrong?" Or someone may say,

"Taking time to share our joys and concerns will make our meetings longer." Someone might even suggest going back to the comforts of Egypt!

Spiritual leaders understand that change has a life cycle, a natural progression of growth. An understanding of that cycle can help ease the resistance people have to new ideas and new ways of thinking. You can read about leading change in another booklet in this series, *What Every Leader Needs to Know About Leading Meetings.* For now think about change as God's way of continuing creation. Acknowledge the fact that it can be disorienting to all of us. However, learning to recognize that change will take place with or without our accepting it and helping others to understand the dynamics and process of change are both important skills for spiritual leaders to develop. Be patient. Be persistent and reassuring. Trust God. You are not alone!

Many fine resources have recently been developed to help introduce faith formation into our meeting settings. See the suggested resources at the end of this booklet and check the many leadership helps at www.gbod.org.

Like those looking over the valley to the Promised Land, we are faced with a critical choice as we think about leading the church into the future. Leaders like you who are willing to take on the challenge of spiritual leadership and lead in this new way will help the church find its way to the place where God is leading us into the future.

The benefits of spiritual leadership to God's work, to your own faith journey, and to your local congregation will far exceed any temporary disorientation caused by moving away from activity-based communities and rediscovering faith-forming communities whose mission is to grow disciples for Jesus Christ in order to transform the world!

May God bless you and your local church on your journey as a spiritual leader called to lead God's people into the fullness of God's Kingdom!

Some Final Reflection

1. List three significant things you have learned by reading this booklet.

2. How can you put these new insights into practice in your life today?

3. Write a prayer for yourself that asks God's help for strength and courage as you answer the call to be a

spiritual leader. Come back from time to time and reread your prayer.

_____

_____

_____

_____

_____

_____

_____

_____

_____

_____

_____

4. How will you share the ideas you have gathered by reading this booklet with the people you lead?

_____

_____

_____

_____

_____

_____

Other Helpful Resources

Websites

Discipleship Resources (www.discipleshipresources.org)

On this online bookstore related to the General Board of Discipleship you can order additional copies of this booklet and other booklets in the *What Every Leader Needs to Know About* ... series. In addition you will find a variety of practical helps and ministry solutions to assist you in your work to fulfill your church's mission through worship, stewardship, evangelism, small-group studies, Christian education and formation, age-level ministries, Wesleyan theology, and other leadership interests.

The Upper Room (www.upperroom.org)

The major focus of resources from The Upper Room, a division of the General Board of Discipleship, is spiritual formation. The Upper Room offers devotional guides such as *The Upper Room,* magazines, books, and studies for individuals or for small groups who want to participate in spiritual formation.

Cokesbury (www.cokesbury.com)

Go to Cokesbury when you are looking for curriculum resources for your Sunday school or official United Methodist resources such as *The Book of Discipline, The Book of Resolutions, The United Methodist Book of Worship,* or *The United Methodist Hymnal.* At the Cokesbury website you will also find a variety of books for developing leadership skills and for leading congregations, not only from United Methodist sources but also from diverse publishers representing many theological views.

United Methodist Communications (www.umcom.org)

Go to UMCom to find information and resources for the Igniting Ministries program; audio and visual materials from EcuFilm for use in Sunday school, Bible studies, and group discussions; help in designing a website for your church; official program calendars; and answers to almost any question about the church through InfoServ.

A Magazine for Leaders

Interpreter, published eight times a year by United Methodist Communications (615-742-5107 or www.interpretermagazine.org).

Job Descriptions

Guidelines for Leading Your Congregation, a series of booklets describing leadership tasks and functions of a variety of groups in the local congregation (800-672-1789 or www.cokesbury.com).

Job Descriptions and Leadership Training for Local Church Leaders (Discipleship Resources, 2004). A collection of single-sheet summaries describing numerous leadership and committee positions that a person may hold in a local congregation (800-972-0433 or www.discipleshipresources.org).

Telephone Consultants

Curric-U-Phone, for help in selecting and using curriculum resources (800-251-8591).

InfoServ, for answers to questions about The United Methodist Church and its ministries (800-251-8140).

Books

Communion, Community, Commonweal: Readings for Spiritual Leadership, edited by John S. Mogabgab (Upper Room Books, 1995). A fine series of writings aimed at ways leaders can grow spiritually. Themes such as listening, remembering, celebrating, communicating, and guiding are discussed to help leaders see how a strong spiritual center ignites others to discover their spiritual centers as well.

Cultivating Christian Community, by Thomas R. Hawkins (Discipleship Resources, 2001). Identifies six qualities of Christian community and offers small-group leaders help as they incorporate these qualities into the life of their group.

Each One a Minister: Using God's Gifts for Ministry, revised edition, by William J. Carter (Discipleship Resources, 2002). Encourages readers to discover God's call to ministry in their own lives and assists congregations as they identify and deploy members for ministry.

Equipped for Every Good Work: Building a Gifts-Based Church, by Dan R. Dick and Barbara Miller (Discipleship Resources, 2001). Describes a four-tool process that can help identify and develop spiritual gifts, spirituality types, interaction styles, and working preferences for each member of your congregation.

FaithQuest: A Journey Toward Congregational Transformation, by Dan R. Dick (Discipleship Resources, 2002). Designed primarily as a Bible study for church leaders, but can also be used by individual leaders who want to learn more about how to lead the church into the future.

Listening to God: Spiritual Formation in the Congregation, by John Ackerman (Alban Institute, 2001). Explores how Christian community begins and grows and how we can nurture ourselves and others through spirit-centered leadership.

Staying Focused: Building Ministry Teams for Christian Formation, by M. Anne Burnette Hook and Shirley F. Clement (Discipleship Resources, 2002). Practical tools for church leaders to engage committees and ministry teams in worship, prayer, and Scripture study.